CONTENTS

Words that look like <u>this</u> are explained in the glossary on page 31.

WELCOME
TO THE
DISASTER ZONE

History is full of grisly stories and weird tales... and a lot of death. From the battlefield to the home, from rich royals to those who didn't have much money at all, people in the past got up to some pretty strange stuff during their lives. So it makes perfect sense for some of those people's lives to have ended in ways that were just as strange.

Around seven percent of all the people who have ever lived are alive right now. How cool is that? You know what that means... there are loads of deaths to choose from!

ATROCIOUS ANIMALS

RIP

Written by
Mignonne
Gunasekara

Designed by
Jasmine Pointer

BookLife PUBLISHING

©2020
BookLife Publishing Ltd.
King's Lynn
Norfolk PE30 4LS

All rights reserved.
Printed in Malaysia.

A catalogue record for this book is available from the British Library.

ISBN: 978-1-83927-814-3

Written by:
Mignonne Gunasekara

Edited by:
John Wood

Designed by:
Jasmine Pointer

PHOTO CREDITS

All images are courtesy of Shutterstock.com, unless otherwise specified. With thanks to Getty Images, Thinkstock Photo and iStockphoto. Background texture throughout – Abstracto. Gravestone throughout – MaryValery. Front Cover – ONYXprj. 5 – dptro, YummyBuum, Nipun Kundu. 6 – hvostik, Cosmic_Design, Panptys, Slowga. 7 – Anastasios71, ONYXprj. 8 – vangelis aragiannis, Viacheslav Lopatin, Darth_Vector. 9 – ariy, Lefteris Papaulakis, Eroshka, matrioshka. 10 – Strilets, bartamarabara, Maglara. 11 – Vertyr. 12 – Nicku, National Library of Scotland [CC0], Oxy_gen, Paragorn Dangsombroon. 13 – Royal Air Force official photographer [Public domain], Bodor Tivadar, Maquiladora, Anatolir, ArtMalivanov. 14 – Dim Tik. 15 – Pavel L Photo and Video, 1507kot. 16 – Greenshed [Public domain], Artist: D'Aveline (French artist, late 17th and early 18th century) [Public domain]. 17 – Public Domain, https://commons.wikimedia.org/w/index.php?curid=584067, Anan Kaewkhammul, Maike Hildebrandt, HappyPictures. 18 – andrey oleynik. 19 – PsyComa. 20 – uzuri, Everett Historical, Maquiladora. 21 – Charles Chusseau-Flaviens [Public domain], The Official Site of the Greek Royal Family [Public domain], Milan M. 23 – delcarmat, Maquiladora, gubernat. 24 – vchal, Plotitsyna NiNa. 25 – Hoika Mikhail, Everett - Art. 26 – LOVE YOU. 27 – Peter Maerky. 28 – V_E, Svetlana Foote, MarGi, svtdesign. 29 – Sarah2, Pogorelova Olga, Dwra.* – U.S. work public domain in the U.S. for unspecified reason but presumably because it was published in the U.S. before 1924. Additional illustrations by Jasmine Pointer.

In this book, we are going to look at the stories of six people who were taken out by atrocious animals. Whether it was pigs on the run, monkeys on the loose or tigers pushed to their limits, we'll find out about the many animal-related ways in which these unfortunate people met their disastrous ends.

INTO THE DISASTER ZONE WE GO . . .

Throughout history, there have been lots of names and sayings that mean someone has died.

Here are a few
of the weird ones:

Kicked the bucket
Bit the dust
Met their maker
Six feet under
Food for worms
Pushing up daisies

AESCHYLUS

Aeschylus was a famous <u>playwright</u> in ancient Greece. Legend says that he'd heard of a <u>prophecy</u> that said he would be killed by a falling object. To stop this coming true, Aeschylus spent as much time as he could outside, where he thought there would be no objects that could fall on him. But nowhere was safe for Aeschylus. Even outside, something did fall on... and kill him. Or rather, something was dropped on him.

An eagle mistook Aeschylus' shiny bald head for a rock and dropped a tortoise on him. Eagles do this to crack open tortoises' shells and eat their insides. We don't know if the tortoise survived this, but we do know that poor Aeschylus didn't.

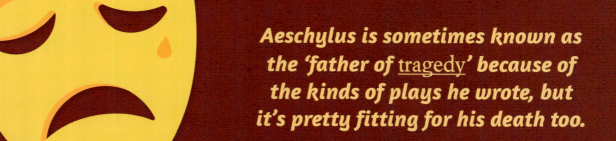

Aeschylus is sometimes known as the 'father of <u>tragedy</u>' because of the kinds of plays he wrote, but it's pretty fitting for his death too.

TO DIE, OR NOT TO DIE

Aeschylus is said to have written around 90 plays, but records of the play titles can only be found for 80 of them. Only seven complete tragedies out of the 90 are still around today.

AESCHYLUS' INFLUENCE

Aeschylus

Many people think of Aeschylus as one of the most important playwrights of all time because of the changes he made to how plays were written and performed. Before Aeschylus,

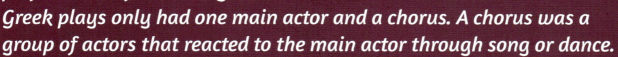

Greek plays only had one main actor and a chorus. A chorus was a group of actors that reacted to the main actor through song or dance.

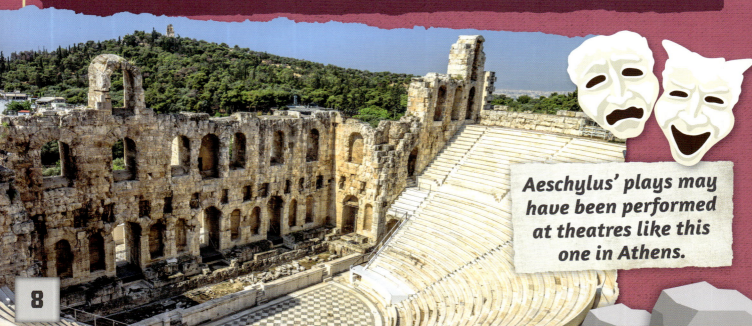

Aeschylus' plays may have been performed at theatres like this one in Athens.

The main actor used to play every character in the story. They would show the audience that they had changed character by wearing a different mask for each one. Aeschylus is thought of as the first person to bring in a second main actor. Now the two main actors could talk to each other and have a conversation. This added more drama to the story.

Ancient Greek theatre masks

Aeschylus wanted the audience to think about why things happened. Did characters get treated fairly? Were the gods mean for no reason?

Aeschylus is also remembered for making costumes and stage scenery much more detailed. His plays were about personal and religious problems, or problems in society. They made people ask questions about life.

Aeschylus wrote plays about characters from Greek mythology.

ELEAZAR AVARAN

Eleazar Avaran was the son of Mattathias, a man who started a <u>rebellion</u> against King Antiochus IV. Antiochus was trying to destroy the Jewish religion and make everyone worship Greek gods instead. When Mattathias died, Eleazar's brother, Judas Maccabeus, took over as leader of the rebellion. Judas managed to take Jerusalem back from Antiochus' control in 164 BC. However, there was a part of the city that was still under Greek control, and Judas wanted to drive them out.

During the battle, Eleazar thought he spotted the war elephant that the Greek king was riding. Eleazar rushed over and stuck his spear into the elephant's belly… the elephant collapsed on top of him and crushed him to death.

Eleazar's side didn't win this battle, but the rebellion is important to Jewish people and is remembered during <u>Hanukkah</u>.

BEASTS IN BATTLE

For centuries, animals of all sizes have been used in war. Aside from fighting, they had many other jobs. Horses were used to carry food, medicine and weapons, and to take injured soldiers to hospital.

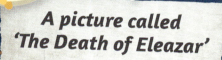

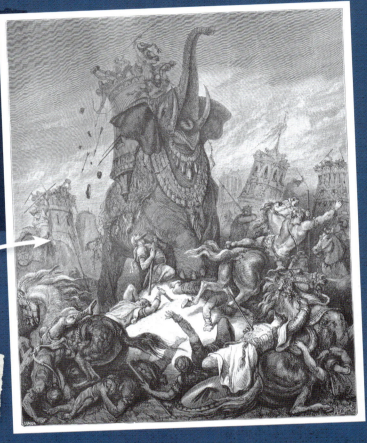

A picture called 'The Death of Eleazar'

Dogs were trained to find and help wounded soldiers on the battlefield. These 'casualty dogs' carried medicine for the soldiers to use, and led rescuers to soldiers who couldn't walk to safety. Dogs have an incredible sense of smell, which has helped them to sniff out and track down hidden bombs in many wars.

A World War One messenger dog

Horses used to be used all the time in wars, especially before <u>World War One</u>. Nowadays other things are used, such as tanks.

PRIVATE... PIGEON?

Carrier pigeons were used to send messages, especially to and from the battlefield. Pigeons have an amazing ability to find their way home from wherever they are, so their nests had to be where a message needed to get to. Over 9 out of 10 messages sent by pigeon during World War One were delivered successfully.

A member of the Royal Air Force holding a carrier pigeon

A pigeon called Cher Ami was awarded a medal for her services during World War One. She delivered her last message even after being shot. The message saved the lives of nearly 200 American soldiers.

Carrying such important information made pigeons targets for the enemy – there are even records of pigeons becoming prisoners of war!

A carrier pigeon

HANNAH TWYNNOY

Not much is known about Hannah Twynnoy's life or death. According to a <u>memorial plaque</u> that has now gone missing, she used to work as a barmaid at the White Lion pub in Malmesbury, England. One day, a travelling <u>menagerie</u> came to town and they set up all their animals in the pub's yard. One of their attractions was a tiger. The story goes that Hannah kept annoying the tiger, even though she was warned not to. At some point, the tiger managed to escape and ended up attacking Hannah.

There is a mystery surrounding Hannah's death. Hannah had a nice gravestone, which was expensive at the time. However, Hannah was not from a rich family... so who paid for it?

Hannah may have been the first person to be killed by a tiger in Britain.

CROUCHING TIGER, ANNOYING HANNAH

Although we will never know for sure, it is most likely that the Church paid for Hannah's grave.

Hannah's gravestone

The poem on her gravestone reads:
In bloom of Life
She's snatchd from hence,
She had not room
To make defence;
For Tyger fierce
Took Life away.
And here she lies
In a bed of Clay,
Until the Resurrection Day.

MENAGERIE MADNESS

People have used animals for entertainment throughout history. The Romans used to make animals fight and perform at the Colosseum. Bear-baiting, where bears are made to fight dogs, was popular in Elizabethan London.

Louis XIV's menagerie at the palace of Versailles

Wealthy people, such as royals, often had their own private menageries. They collected exotic, rare or impressive animals as status symbols.

Compared to bear-baiting, travelling menageries seemed quite tame. They really started to become more popular in the 18th and 19th centuries, as more people travelled around the world and brought back new and interesting animals to England, Europe and the US. Menageries were seen as educational as well as entertaining because people could see exotic animals up close.

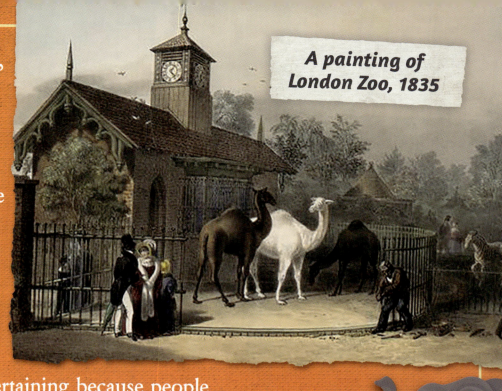

A painting of London Zoo, 1835

Among the animals on show in the Royal Menagerie at the Tower of London were lions, an elephant, a polar bear and a leopard.

At first, menageries just showed animals in cages or pens, but people eventually became bored of just looking at them. Menageries then started making the animals perform to bring the crowds back in.

ALEXANDER I OF GREECE

Alexander came to rule Greece when he was 24 years old. With him as king, Greece hoped to expand their borders… but they never got the chance, as Alexander was killed in a sudden monkey attack. Alexander had been walking his dog, Fritz, through the gardens of Tatoi Palace when Fritz was attacked by a pair of pet monkeys. Alexander tried to break up the fight, and the monkeys turned on him.

Alexander was bitten, but he didn't think it was very serious. He just got bandaged up and went about his day. However, by that night, he had developed an <u>infection</u>. Over the next few days, the infection spread around his body until it was too late to save him.

The monkeys that attacked Fritz were a pair of Barbary macaques that belonged to someone who worked at the palace.

BORN: Athens, Greece
DIED: Tatoi, Greece
CLAIM TO FAME: King of Greece from 1917–1920
DEATH BY: Macaque

IT'S JUST A FLESH WOUND

Little did anyone realise that Barbary macaques would go on to change history.

Barbary macaque

Following Alexander's death, his father, Constantine I, was brought back to rule Greece. Constantine had already been king before, from 1913 until 1917. He'd been forced to leave the throne by Allied forces during World War One. This was because they wanted Greece to fight in the war on their side, and Constantine didn't want to do that. Alexander was happy to fight with the Allies.

British soldiers during World War One

The Allied forces of World War One were countries that fought together against Germany and its supporters, which were called the Central Powers. The Allies included Britain, France and Russia.

As a reward for fighting on the Allied side, the Allies offered to help Greece expand their borders. Greece sent their army into neighbouring areas to try and take more land, and things were going well... until Alexander died and Constantine returned.

Alexander I of Greece

Constantine I of Greece

Winston Churchill, one of the UK's most famous prime ministers, seemed to think the monkeys had a lot to answer for.

The Allies didn't want to help anymore. However, Greece decided to keep pushing forward into places such as Anatolia without them. The Greek forces were now no match for the Turkish forces that were defending these areas and by 1922, Greece had been defeated and driven away.

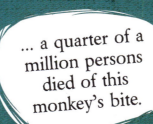

... a quarter of a million persons died of this monkey's bite.

HERACLITUS

Heraclitus was a Greek <u>philosopher</u>. People annoyed him so much that he tried to get as far away as possible from them by going to live in the mountains. The story goes that he didn't have a very good diet up there and eventually became sick. Heraclitus believed the cure for his illness was to cover himself in cow dung.

He hoped that the warmth of the cow dung would draw the illness out of his body. However, the dung dried out and became a solid cast around his body – Heraclitus was trapped! As if things couldn't get any worse, some people say that a pack of hungry wild dogs then appeared. Heraclitus made the perfect snack for them.

Heraclitus is known as the 'weeping philosopher' because of how sad he was, and as the 'dark philosopher' because his philosophy could be quite difficult to understand.

BORN: Ephesus, Turkey
DIED: Ephesus, Turkey
CLAIM TO FAME: Grumpy guts philosopher
DEATH BY: Dogs' dinner

I'm telling you, this will work!

540–480 BC

DROPSY, DUNG AND DOGS

While Heraclitus was roaming around the mountains, the only things he ate were apparently grass and plants. No wonder he got sick! Heraclitus' illness was called dropsy, which is when water gets collected in the body where it shouldn't be. It can be quite painful, which may explain why Heraclitus was not thinking straight.

Dropsy is now known as oedema.

Heraclitus challenged the philosophers that came before him, and the philosophers of his time. He helped push philosophy in a new direction.

MR KNOW-IT-ALL

The ruins of the Temple of Artemis at Ephesus

Heraclitus is said to have written all his philosophical ideas down in one book, which he then left at the Temple of Artemis at Ephesus. The book was mostly lost – just over 100 <u>fragments</u> of it are still around today.

From these fragments, people have been able to work out some of the things that Heraclitus wrote about in his philosophy. One of his most famous ideas is that things are always changing. He called this 'flux'.

Artemis

Artemis is the Greek goddess of hunting, wild animals and the Moon. Maybe she should have got those wild dogs to leave Heraclitus alone!

A painting of Heraclitus

A second idea of Heraclitus' is that opposites go hand in hand with each other, such as being young and being old, and being awake and being asleep. He called this the 'unity of opposites'. He said that opposites were connected and were both important. They made the universe balanced.

PHILIP OF FRANCE

On the orders of his father, Louis VI, Philip was made joint king of France alongside Louis himself. Philip was only 13 at the time but Louis had high hopes that Philip would be a good king.

However, Philip didn't get a chance to prove him right. He died just two years later after running into a black pig. Philip and a group of friends were riding their horses through the streets of Paris when a black pig appeared out of a dung heap in front of them. It ran towards the riders and Philip's horse tripped over it. Philip was sent flying from his saddle and ended up dying of his injuries.

Philip wasn't the best-behaved co-king during his short reign. He was apparently quite arrogant and refused to listen to advice.

SANITATION SITUATION

So, the pig that tripped up Philip's horse jumped out of a pile of dung. But why were there piles of dung lying in the road in Paris in 1131?

At that point in history, people didn't know how important it was to get rid of waste properly. As long as waste was out of the way, they thought that it wasn't a problem. This meant that a popular way to get rid of waste was to dump it in rivers. This is a bad idea because people used the water from those same rivers to cook and clean. This often spread disease.

There even used to be public toilets on London Bridge. They dropped their waste into the river Thames below! Yuck.

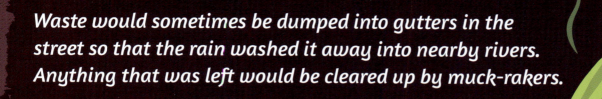

Waste would sometimes be dumped into gutters in the street so that the rain washed it away into nearby rivers. Anything that was left would be cleared up by muck-rakers.

THE GREAT STINK

Muck-rakers were people who were paid to clear up waste from the streets and take it to dumpsites outside the city.

In the summer of 1858, London was hit by the most horrible stink. The hot sunshine was baking all the poo that had been dumped into the Thames for years, and the smell was unbearable. Politicians were so grossed out that they quickly ordered a new sewer system to be built in London so this would never happen again.

Chamber pots were kept in bedrooms. People would go to the toilet in them, then empty them into gutters or <u>cesspits</u>.

29

TIMELINE OF DEATH

HERACLITUS
480 BC

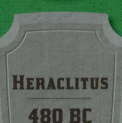

AESCHYLUS
456 BC

ELEAZAR AVARAN
163 BC

ALEXANDER I OF GREECE
1920

HANNAH TWYNNOY
1703

PHILIP OF FRANCE
1131

GLOSSARY

BC	meaning 'before Christ', it is used to mark dates that occurred before the starting year of most calendars
CESSPITS	holes in the ground that collect human waste
COLOSSEUM	a grand theatre built by the ancient Romans
EXOTIC	from a new or foreign place
FRAGMENTS	a small piece that has been broken off or separated from something whole
GREEK MYTHOLOGY	stories to do with the gods, heroes and lives of ancient Greeks
HANUKKAH	an eight-day-long Jewish holiday that celebrates the Temple of Jerusalem being taken back from Antiochus IV
INFECTION	when a wound or body part is diseased because bacteria or a virus has got inside it
MEMORIAL PLAQUE	a plate, usually of metal or stone, that is fixed to a wall or other structure to remind people of a person or event
MENAGERIE	a collection of animals, usually for entertainment or research purposes
PHILOSOPHER	a person who studies the nature of knowledge, reality and existence
PLAYWRIGHT	a person who writes plays
PROPHECY	something that says what is going to happen in the future
REBELLION	when a group or individual fights back against the rules of somebody who is in control
SOCIETY	a collection of people living together
STAGE SCENERY	items and backgrounds that are used on stage to make it look like a certain time or place
STATUS SYMBOLS	things that show how rich or important someone is
TRAGEDY	plays that are about something sad with no happy ending
WORLD WAR ONE	a war fought between 1914 and 1918

INDEX